THEORY
OF SUPPLY

Decoding Crypto Money Making Opportunities

Table of Contents

Cryptocurrency Faucets: Earn small amounts of various cryptocurrencies by completing simple tasks or captcha on faucet websites.

Developing and Selling NFTs: Create and sell non-fungible tokens (NFTs) representing digital assets like art, music, or collectibles.

Running a Masternode: Operate a full node in certain blockchain networks and earn rewards for supporting the network's functionalities.

Crypto Freelancing: Offer your skills and services in exchange for cryptocurrencies on freelancing platforms that accept digital currencies.

Crypto Affiliate Marketing: Promote cryptocurrency products or services through affiliate programs, earning commissions on successful referrals.

The Art of Trading Cryptocurrencies: Profiting from Price Fluctuations

In the ever-evolving landscape of finance, the rise of cryptocurrencies has introduced a myriad of opportunities for individuals seeking to engage in the dynamic world of trading. One of the primary methods enthusiasts and investors use to capitalize on the volatile nature of digital assets is through trading cryptocurrencies on various exchanges. This article will delve into the essentials of trading cryptocurrencies, exploring the strategies, risks, and key considerations for those looking to navigate this fast-paced market.

Understanding the Basics

Before delving into the intricacies of cryptocurrency trading, it's crucial to grasp the fundamentals. Cryptocurrencies are digital or virtual currencies that utilize cryptography for security and operate on decentralized networks based on blockchain technology. Trading involves buying and selling these digital assets on various cryptocurrency exchanges with the aim of profiting from the price fluctuations.

Choosing the Right Exchange

The first step in cryptocurrency trading is selecting a reputable and secure exchange. These platforms act as intermediaries, facilitating the buying and selling of digital assets. Popular exchanges like

Coinbase, Binance, and Kraken provide a user-friendly interface, a variety of listed assets, and robust security measures. Traders must consider factors such as liquidity, fees, security, and available trading pairs when choosing an exchange.

Developing a Trading Strategy

Successful cryptocurrency trading requires a well-defined strategy. Traders can adopt various approaches, including day trading, swing trading, and long-term investing. Day traders capitalize on short-term price movements, executing multiple trades within a single day. Swing traders aim to profit from price "swings" over a period of days or weeks, while long-term investors hold assets for more extended periods, often based on fundamental analysis.

Technical and Fundamental Analysis

Technical analysis involves studying price charts, trading volumes, and historical market data to make informed decisions. Traders use technical indicators, such as moving averages, Relative Strength Index (RSI), and Bollinger Bands, to identify trends and potential entry or exit points. On the other hand, fundamental analysis focuses on evaluating a cryptocurrency's underlying factors, such as technology, team, partnerships, and market demand.

Risk Management

Trading cryptocurrencies inherently involves risk due to market volatility. Implementing effective risk management strategies is paramount to safeguarding investments. This includes setting stop-loss orders to limit potential losses, diversifying a portfolio across different assets, and only investing what one can afford to lose. Successful traders understand the importance of preserving capital and avoiding emotional decision-making.

Staying Informed

Cryptocurrency markets are influenced by a myriad of factors, including regulatory developments, technological advancements, and macroeconomic trends. Staying informed about these factors is essential for making informed trading decisions. Traders often follow cryptocurrency news sources, participate in online communities, and track social media channels to gauge market sentiment and potential catalysts.

Overcoming Challenges

While the potential for profit is enticing, traders must also navigate challenges inherent in the cryptocurrency market. These challenges include price manipulation, security concerns, and regulatory uncertainties. By staying vigilant, conducting thorough research, and being aware of potential pitfalls, traders can mitigate risks and make informed decisions.

Conclusion

In conclusion, trading cryptocurrencies offers a unique opportunity for individuals to capitalize on the volatility of digital assets. Success in this space requires a combination of technical knowledge, strategic planning, and a disciplined approach to risk management. As with any investment, it's crucial to conduct thorough research, stay informed about market developments, and continually adapt to the ever-changing dynamics of the cryptocurrency landscape. Whether you're a seasoned trader or a newcomer to the world of cryptocurrencies, embracing a cautious and informed approach is key to navigating the exciting and sometimes tumultuous waters of cryptocurrency trading.

Unveiling the World of Cryptocurrency Mining: A Guide to Setting Up Profitable Mining Operations

In the realm of cryptocurrencies, mining stands out as a fundamental process that not only validates transactions but also allows individuals to earn rewards in the form of newly created coins. This article will unravel the intricacies of mining operations, exploring the essentials of setting up and operating mining rigs to partake in the decentralized validation of transactions.

Understanding Cryptocurrency Mining

At its core, cryptocurrency mining is the process by which transactions are verified and added to a blockchain. This verification is achieved through solving complex mathematical problems, a task performed by specialized hardware known as mining rigs. In return for their computational efforts, miners are rewarded with a certain amount of newly created coins, depending on the specific cryptocurrency's reward structure.

Choosing the Right Cryptocurrency to Mine

Before embarking on a mining venture, it's crucial to select a cryptocurrency that aligns with your goals and resources. Bitcoin, Ethereum, and Litecoin are among the popular choices, each with its unique mining algorithms and reward mechanisms. Factors such as mining difficulty, potential profitability, and hardware compatibility should be considered when making this decision.

Selecting Mining Hardware

The backbone of any mining operation is the hardware. Mining rigs come in various shapes and sizes, ranging from simple CPU and GPU setups to more sophisticated ASIC (Application-Specific Integrated Circuit) machines designed for specific algorithms. The choice of hardware depends on the targeted cryptocurrency and the miner's budget. ASICs, while expensive, often offer higher hash rates and energy efficiency compared to traditional GPU setups.

Setting Up the Mining Rig

Once the hardware is acquired, the next step is setting up the mining rig. This involves configuring the necessary software, connecting to the mining pool, and ensuring proper cooling mechanisms are in place. Mining pools, where multiple miners combine their computational power to increase the chances of successfully validating transactions and earning rewards, are a common choice for small-scale miners.

Joining a Mining Pool

Mining independently can be a daunting task due to the increasing difficulty of mining algorithms. Joining a mining pool allows miners to collaborate and share rewards based on their contributed computational power. Popular mining pools for various cryptocurrencies include Slush Pool, F2Pool, and Ethermine. Pool selection should consider factors such as fees, payout frequency, and reputation.

Electricity Costs and Profitability

Mining operations consume a significant amount of electricity, and thus, understanding the associated costs is crucial for determining profitability. Miners need to assess their electricity rates, hardware efficiency, and potential revenue based on current market prices. Tools like mining calculators can aid in estimating profitability by considering factors such as hash rate, power consumption, and the current block reward.

Staying Informed and Adapting

Cryptocurrency mining is a dynamic landscape influenced by technological advancements, market trends, and network upgrades. Miners must stay informed about changes in algorithms, hardware innovations, and any potential shifts in the cryptocurrency landscape. Adapting to these changes is essential for maintaining profitability and sustainability in the mining venture.

Navigating Challenges and Risks

Mining operations are not without challenges. Factors like regulatory uncertainties, hardware obsolescence, and market volatility can impact the profitability of mining ventures. Miners should be prepared to navigate these challenges with resilience, staying attuned to industry developments and adjusting their strategies accordingly.

Conclusion

In conclusion, cryptocurrency mining offers a unique avenue for individuals to actively participate in the decentralized validation of transactions while earning rewards in the form of newly created coins. Setting up and operating mining rigs requires careful consideration of various factors, from choosing the right cryptocurrency and hardware to managing electricity costs and staying informed about industry developments. Aspiring miners should approach this endeavor with a blend of technical know-how, strategic planning, and a willingness to adapt to the ever-evolving landscape of cryptocurrency mining.

Unlocking Passive Income: A Guide to Staking Cryptocurrencies in Proof-of-Stake Networks

In the ever-expanding universe of cryptocurrencies, staking has emerged as a compelling avenue for investors to not only support blockchain networks but also earn rewards in the process. This article delves into the world of staking cryptocurrencies, focusing on participation in proof-of-stake networks and the mechanisms involved in locking up coins to secure and validate transactions.

Understanding Proof-of-Stake (PoS)

Proof-of-Stake is a consensus algorithm used by certain blockchain networks to achieve distributed consensus. Unlike Proof-of-Work (PoW), which relies on computational power and miners, PoS selects validators based on the amount of cryptocurrency they hold and are willing to "stake" as collateral. Stakers are chosen to create new blocks and validate transactions based on their stake, fostering a more energy-efficient and environmentally friendly network.

Choosing Staking-Friendly Cryptocurrencies

Not all cryptocurrencies utilize PoS, so the first step is to identify those that do. Prominent examples include Ethereum 2.0, Cardano, Tezos, and Polkadot. Each of these networks employs variations of PoS, offering different staking mechanisms, reward structures, and entry requirements for participants.

Acquiring and Staking Cryptocurrencies

To stake, one must acquire a certain amount of the cryptocurrency associated with the PoS network. The minimum staking requirement varies among different networks. Once acquired, participants lock up their coins in a designated wallet or smart contract. This process, commonly referred to as "staking," demonstrates commitment to the network and allows users to be considered for the validation of transactions.

Choosing Between Staking Pools and Solo Staking

Stakers have the option to participate individually or join staking pools. In solo staking, individuals bear the responsibility of maintaining a node and securing the network. Staking pools, on the other hand, involve multiple participants combining their stakes, increasing the chances of being chosen to validate transactions. Pools distribute rewards proportionally among participants based on their contribution to the pool's total stake.

Earning Rewards and Compound Interest

The primary incentive for staking cryptocurrencies is the opportunity to earn rewards. Validators, whether solo or part of a pool, receive newly created coins or transaction fees as compensation for their participation in securing the network. Stakers can choose to compound their rewards by reinvesting them into additional stakes, leading to a compounding effect that enhances overall returns over time.

Risk Mitigation and Security

While staking is generally considered a low-risk activity compared to other forms of cryptocurrency engagement, participants should be aware of potential risks. Network upgrades, vulnerabilities, and market fluctuations can impact staking rewards and the overall value of the staked assets. Diligent research, staying informed about network developments, and employing secure staking practices are crucial for risk mitigation.

Staying Informed about Network Upgrades and Changes

Proof-of-Stake networks undergo upgrades and changes to enhance functionality, security, and scalability. Stakers must stay informed about these developments to adapt their strategies accordingly. Network upgrades can introduce changes to staking parameters, reward structures, and other critical aspects that affect the staking experience.

Conclusion

Staking cryptocurrencies in proof-of-stake networks presents a compelling opportunity for investors seeking passive income while actively contributing to the security and decentralization of blockchain networks. As the cryptocurrency landscape evolves, staking continues to gain prominence as a sustainable and eco-friendly alternative to traditional mining. By understanding the nuances of PoS, choosing suitable cryptocurrencies, and actively managing staking participation, enthusiasts can unlock the potential for long-term rewards and actively participate in the vibrant ecosystem of decentralized finance.

Navigating the Crypto Frontier: A Comprehensive Guide to Initial Coin Offerings (ICOs)

In the dynamic realm of cryptocurrencies, Initial Coin Offerings (ICOs) have emerged as a revolutionary method for new projects to secure funding while providing investors with a unique opportunity to participate in the early stages of innovation. This article aims to shed light on the intricacies of ICOs, exploring how individuals can invest in new cryptocurrency projects during their fundraising phase and potentially reap rewards as these projects evolve.

Understanding ICOs

An Initial Coin Offering is a fundraising method employed by new cryptocurrency projects to raise capital for development. In an ICO, a project issues its own native tokens or coins, which investors can purchase using established cryptocurrencies like Bitcoin or Ethereum. In return for their investment, participants receive a share of the project's tokens, essentially becoming early backers with the potential for future gains.

Researching ICO Projects

With numerous ICOs being launched, thorough research is paramount before deciding to invest. Investigate the project's whitepaper, which outlines its goals, technology, and tokenomics. Assess the team's experience, partnerships, and the problem the project aims to solve. Analyze the token distribution plan, roadmap, and any existing prototypes or Minimum Viable Products (MVPs) to gauge the project's viability.

Participating in ICOs

To participate in an ICO, investors typically need to register on the project's official website and follow the instructions provided. The contribution is made in the form of established cryptocurrencies, and in return, investors receive the newly created project tokens. It's crucial to follow the specific guidelines outlined by the project to ensure a secure and successful participation process.

Risks and Considerations

While ICOs offer a unique investment opportunity, they come with inherent risks. The cryptocurrency market is known for its volatility, and ICO projects are no exception. Investors should be aware of potential pitfalls such as regulatory uncertainties, market sentiment shifts, and the risk of project failure. Diversification and only investing what one can afford to lose are key principles to mitigate risks associated with ICO investments.

Post-ICO: Managing Tokens and Tracking Progress

After the ICO concludes, investors receive their tokens, and the project enters its development phase. It's crucial to secure and manage these tokens using secure wallets compatible with the project's blockchain. Additionally, staying informed about the project's progress, updates, and achieving milestones is essential for making informed decisions about holding, selling, or further participation in the project's ecosystem.

Regulatory Landscape

The regulatory environment surrounding ICOs varies globally. Some jurisdictions embrace ICOs, while others impose strict regulations. Investors must be aware of the legal implications in their respective regions and adhere to compliance standards. Regulatory clarity is an ongoing aspect of the cryptocurrency space, and changes in legislation can impact the ICO landscape.

Secondary Markets and Token Liquidity

Investors often seek liquidity for their ICO tokens, and secondary markets, such as cryptocurrency exchanges, play a crucial role in facilitating trading. Tracking the token's market performance, understanding liquidity conditions, and being mindful of market sentiment are important considerations for those looking to buy or sell ICO tokens on secondary markets.

In conclusion, Initial Coin Offerings represent a transformative way for investors to engage with nascent cryptocurrency projects and potentially participate in their growth story. While ICOs have fueled innovation and provided substantial returns for early backers, the landscape requires careful consideration and due diligence. By researching projects thoroughly, understanding the risks, and staying informed about regulatory developments, investors can navigate the ICO space with prudence, contributing to the vibrant and ever-evolving world of cryptocurrency investment.

Empowering Participation: A Guide to Delegated Proof-of-Stake (DPoS) Networks

Delegated Proof-of-Stake (DPoS) stands out as an innovative consensus algorithm within the cryptocurrency space, offering individuals the opportunity to actively engage in network governance. This article explores the intricacies of DPoS, elucidating how participants can contribute to DPoS systems by voting for network validators and earning rewards in return.

Understanding Delegated Proof-of-Stake (DPoS)

DPoS is a consensus algorithm that prioritizes efficiency and scalability in blockchain networks. Unlike traditional Proof-of-Work (PoW) systems, DPoS relies on a select group of validators, known as delegates or witnesses, chosen by the community through a voting process. These delegates are responsible for validating transactions and producing new blocks. DPoS aims to streamline decision-making and enhance network throughput by allowing token holders to vote for trustworthy and competent validators.

Choosing DPoS Networks

Several prominent blockchain networks employ DPoS, each with its unique features and governance structures. Examples include EOS, TRON, and Lisk. When considering participation, individuals should research and choose a DPoS network aligned with their values, goals, and technological preferences.

Acquiring and Staking Tokens

To participate in DPoS, individuals typically need to acquire and stake the native tokens of the respective blockchain network. Staking involves locking up a certain amount of tokens as collateral to demonstrate commitment and gain voting power. The more tokens staked, the greater the influence participants wield in the delegate election process.

Voting for Delegates

DPoS networks enable token holders to vote for delegates they trust to validate transactions and maintain network integrity. The voting process is a key aspect of DPoS governance, allowing the community to influence the composition of the validating nodes.

Voters can review delegate proposals, assess their technical competence, and consider their contributions to the network before casting their votes.

Earning Rewards through Delegation

One of the primary incentives for participating in DPoS is the opportunity to earn rewards through delegation. Delegates receive compensation in the form of newly created tokens or transaction fees for their role in securing the network. Token holders who participate in the voting process can share in these rewards proportionally based on the number of tokens they have staked.

Dynamic Governance and Adaptability

DPoS networks often implement dynamic governance mechanisms, allowing token holders to propose and vote on protocol upgrades, parameter changes, and other network improvements. This democratic approach fosters adaptability and ensures that the network evolves in response to the community's consensus.

Risk Mitigation and Security

While DPoS provides an efficient consensus mechanism, participants should be aware of potential risks. These include the centralization of power among a small number of delegates, the risk of collusion, and the impact of malicious actors. Diligent research, ongoing participation in the community, and staying informed about the network's governance decisions are essential for mitigating these risks.

Staying Informed and Engaged

Active participation in DPoS goes beyond the initial voting process. Stakers and voters should stay informed about network developments, delegate performance, and any proposed changes to the governance structure. Engagement in community forums, discussions, and regular assessments of the network's progress contribute to a healthy and transparent DPoS ecosystem.

Conclusion

In conclusion, Delegated Proof-of-Stake offers a democratic and efficient alternative to traditional consensus algorithms. By participating in DPoS systems, individuals can contribute to network governance, vote for validators they trust, and earn rewards in return. The collaborative nature of DPoS not only enhances decentralization but also empowers the community to shape the future of blockchain networks. As the cryptocurrency space continues to evolve, DPoS stands as a testament to the importance of active engagement and decentralized decision-making in the journey towards a more inclusive and scalable blockchain ecosystem.

Dripping Rewards: Exploring the World of Cryptocurrency Faucets

Cryptocurrency faucets have become a popular entry point for individuals looking to dip their toes into the world of digital assets without a significant upfront investment. This article delves into the concept of cryptocurrency faucets, elucidating how users can earn small amounts of various cryptocurrencies by completing simple tasks or captchas on faucet websites.

Understanding Cryptocurrency Faucets

Cryptocurrency faucets are online platforms that dispense small amounts of digital currencies as rewards for completing straightforward tasks. These tasks often include solving captchas, watching short advertisements, or answering surveys. Faucets serve as a novel way to distribute cryptocurrency to a broad audience, fostering wider adoption and allowing users to accumulate small amounts of various coins.

Choosing Faucets and Ensuring Legitimacy

With numerous faucets available, selecting trustworthy platforms is crucial. Legitimate faucets are transparent about their reward distribution, have a user-friendly interface, and provide clear instructions for completing tasks. Users should be cautious and avoid faucets that request personal information or have suspicious practices.

Completing Tasks for Cryptocurrency Rewards

Participating in cryptocurrency faucets is a straightforward process. Users typically visit the faucet website, complete the specified task (e.g., solving a captcha), and receive a small amount of cryptocurrency as a reward. The frequency of payouts varies among faucets, with some offering rewards at regular intervals, while others may have daily or hourly distribution schedules.

Supported Cryptocurrencies and Wallets

Faucets often distribute a variety of cryptocurrencies, allowing users to diversify their digital asset holdings. Commonly distributed cryptocurrencies include Bitcoin, Ethereum, Litecoin, and more. Users should have a cryptocurrency wallet compatible with the faucets they choose to collect and store their earned tokens securely.

Setting Realistic Expectations

While cryptocurrency faucets provide an accessible way to earn digital assets, users should set realistic expectations. The amounts distributed are typically small, and accumulating significant holdings may take time. Faucets are more about introducing users to the cryptocurrency space than serving as a primary income source.

Security and Privacy Considerations

Maintaining security and privacy is paramount when engaging with cryptocurrency faucets. Users should use secure and reputable wallets to receive rewards. Additionally, it's advisable to employ strong, unique passwords for faucet accounts and avoid sharing sensitive information. Vigilance helps users navigate the online landscape safely.

Exploring Additional Features

Some faucets offer additional features beyond basic tasks, such as referral programs, games, or loyalty bonuses. Referral programs enable users to earn additional rewards by inviting friends to join the faucet. Exploring these features can enhance the overall earning potential and engagement with the faucet platform.

Community and User Forums

Engaging with the community and participating in user forums associated with cryptocurrency faucets can provide valuable insights and tips. Users often share their experiences, discuss new faucet opportunities, and offer advice on maximizing earnings. Active participation in these communities contributes to a supportive and informed faucet experience.

Conclusion

Cryptocurrency faucets represent an intriguing entry point into the world of digital assets, offering users the chance to earn small amounts of various cryptocurrencies through simple tasks. While not a get-rich-quick method, faucets provide an educational and accessible way for individuals to familiarize themselves with cryptocurrencies. By selecting legitimate faucets, prioritizing security, and setting realistic expectations, users can embark on a rewarding journey of incremental cryptocurrency accumulation through these novel online platforms.

Unleashing Digital Creativity: A Guide to Developing and Selling NFTs

In the ever-evolving landscape of the digital economy, non-fungible tokens (NFTs) have emerged as a groundbreaking way for creators to tokenize and monetize their digital assets. This article delves into the world of developing and selling NFTs, exploring the steps involved in creating and marketing unique digital collectibles such as art, music, or other digital assets.

Understanding NFTs

Non-fungible tokens are unique cryptographic tokens that represent ownership of a specific digital asset or piece of content. Unlike cryptocurrencies such as Bitcoin or Ethereum, which are fungible and interchangeable, NFTs are indivisible and distinguishable, making each one unique. This uniqueness is what gives NFTs their value, especially in the realm of digital art, music, and collectibles.

Creating Digital Assets for NFTs

The first step in developing NFTs is to create the digital assets you wish to tokenize. This could be digital artwork, music tracks, virtual real estate, or any other digital content with unique value. Creators often use graphic design software, 3D modeling tools, or other specialized software to produce high-quality and original digital assets.

Choosing the Right Blockchain Platform

NFTs are typically built on blockchain platforms, with Ethereum being the most popular. However, other blockchains like Binance Smart Chain, Flow, and Tezos also support NFTs. Each platform has its own set of characteristics, including transaction costs, environmental impact, and community. Choosing the right platform depends on your preferences, audience, and the specific features offered.

Minting NFTs

Minting is the process of creating NFTs by tokenizing your digital assets on the chosen blockchain. This involves using a smart contract that defines the uniqueness and ownership of your digital asset. Platforms like OpenSea, Mintable, and Rarible simplify the minting process, allowing creators to upload their digital files, set metadata, and mint NFTs with a few clicks.

Setting Ownership and Royalties

When minting NFTs, creators have the option to set ownership parameters and royalties. Ownership settings determine whether the creator retains certain rights to the digital asset even after it's sold. Royalties enable creators to earn a percentage of sales whenever the NFT is resold in the secondary market, providing an ongoing revenue stream.

Marketing and Selling NFTs

Effectively marketing and selling NFTs is crucial for success in the NFT space. Utilize social media platforms, online marketplaces, and NFT-dedicated communities to showcase your work. Building a strong online presence and engaging with potential buyers can create a buzz around your NFTs. Additionally, participating in NFT drops, collaborations, and virtual events can enhance visibility and attract a wider audience.

Securing and Delivering NFTs

After a sale, ensuring a secure and seamless delivery of the NFT to the buyer is essential. Most blockchain platforms and NFT marketplaces handle the technicalities of transferring ownership, but creators should be aware of the process. Providing additional perks such as exclusive content, unlockable features, or physical merchandise can enhance the overall value proposition for buyers.

Navigating Legal and Ethical Considerations

As the NFT space evolves, legal and ethical considerations come to the forefront. Creators should be mindful of intellectual property rights, licensing agreements, and potential disputes. Clear communication with buyers about usage rights and limitations helps establish transparency and prevents misunderstandings.

Conclusion

In conclusion, developing and selling NFTs offers creators a novel way to monetize digital assets and connect with a global audience. By understanding the NFT creation process, choosing the right blockchain platform, and employing effective marketing strategies, creators can unlock the full potential of this transformative digital ecosystem. As the NFT space continues to evolve, embracing innovation, fostering creativity, and navigating ethical considerations will be key to a successful journey in the vibrant world of digital collectibles.

Harnessing Blockchain Infrastructure: A Guide to Running Masternodes for Passive Income

Running a masternode is a compelling venture within the cryptocurrency realm, offering individuals the opportunity to actively contribute to blockchain networks while earning rewards. This article delves into the intricacies of operating a masternode, elucidating how enthusiasts can support network functionalities and receive passive income in return.

Understanding Masternodes

Masternodes are full nodes in a blockchain network that perform additional functions beyond basic transaction verification. These nodes play a crucial role in enhancing the network's performance, security, and scalability. To operate a masternode, participants are typically required to hold a certain amount of the network's native cryptocurrency as collateral, demonstrating a commitment to the ecosystem.

Choosing Blockchain Networks

Various blockchain networks implement masternodes, each with its unique features and reward structures. Examples include Dash, Zcoin, and Horizen. When considering running a masternode, individuals should conduct thorough research to understand the specific requirements, potential returns, and the overall vision of the network they plan to support.

Setting up a Masternode

Setting up a masternode involves several steps, including acquiring the requisite amount of the network's native cryptocurrency, configuring a server, and deploying the masternode software. While the exact process varies depending on the blockchain network, most projects provide comprehensive guides and documentation to assist users in the setup process.

Collateral and Staking Requirements

Masternodes typically require participants to lock up a specific amount of the network's native cryptocurrency as collateral. This collateral serves as a security measure, discouraging malicious behavior and ensuring that masternode operators have a vested interest in the network's success. Participants receive rewards for their service and commitment to maintaining the masternode.

Earning Rewards through Masternodes

The primary incentive for running a masternode is the opportunity to earn rewards. Masternode operators receive a share of the block rewards generated by the network, often in the form of the native cryptocurrency. The reward structure varies among blockchain projects, and some networks implement mechanisms like Proof-of-Service to further ensure masternode operators contribute meaningfully to the network.

Monitoring and Maintaining Masternodes

Successfully running a masternode requires ongoing monitoring and maintenance. Operators need to ensure that their masternode is online and functioning correctly. Additionally, staying informed about network upgrades, participating in governance decisions, and actively engaging with the community contribute to a positive and fruitful masternode experience.

Risk Management and Security

While masternodes offer a passive income stream, operators should be aware of potential risks. Fluctuations in the cryptocurrency market, network vulnerabilities, and changes in project development can impact the profitability of masternodes. Implementing robust security measures, staying informed about network developments, and diversifying investments are key aspects of risk management.

Community Engagement and Governance

Masternode operators often play a role in the governance of blockchain networks. Many projects allow operators to vote on proposals and network upgrades. Active participation in governance discussions and community forums contributes to the decentralization and democratization of decision-making within the blockchain ecosystem.

Conclusion

In conclusion, running a masternode presents a unique opportunity for individuals to actively contribute to blockchain networks while earning passive income. By understanding the requirements of specific blockchain projects, setting up and maintaining masternodes, and staying informed about network developments, operators can navigate this dynamic space with confidence. As the cryptocurrency landscape continues to evolve, the role of masternodes in supporting the infrastructure and governance of blockchain networks remains a fascinating aspect of decentralized ecosystems.

Unleashing Skills for Cryptocurrency: A Freelancer's Guide to Crypto-Based Gig Economy

The intersection of freelancing and cryptocurrencies has opened up a new realm of opportunities for skilled individuals seeking alternative avenues for work and payment. This article explores the concept of crypto freelancing, where individuals can offer their expertise on freelancing platforms that accept digital currencies as a means of exchange.

Understanding Crypto Freelancing

Crypto freelancing involves offering services or skills on freelancing platforms that facilitate transactions in cryptocurrencies. Traditional freelancing platforms like Upwork and Freelancer have expanded to accommodate digital currencies, allowing freelancers to receive payments in Bitcoin, Ethereum, and other cryptocurrencies. This paradigm shift provides freelancers with more financial flexibility and access to a global client base.

Choosing Freelancing Platforms that Accept Cryptocurrencies

To embark on a crypto freelancing journey, freelancers should choose platforms that support cryptocurrency transactions. Websites like Bitwage, CryptoTask, and LaborX specialize in connecting freelancers with clients who are willing to pay in digital currencies. Evaluating the platform's reputation, security features, and available job categories is essential when selecting the right platform.

Listing Services and Setting Rates

Similar to traditional freelancing, crypto freelancers need to create profiles showcasing their skills, experience, and the services they offer. Setting competitive and fair rates in cryptocurrencies is crucial, considering the volatility of digital assets. Clearly defining the scope of services, deliverables, and payment terms ensures transparent communication with potential clients.

Navigating Cryptocurrency Payments

Freelancers on crypto-friendly platforms can specify their preferred digital currency for payments. Once a job is completed, clients transfer the agreed-upon amount in cryptocurrency to the freelancer's wallet. It's essential for freelancers to be familiar with the wallet addresses associated with the cryptocurrencies they accept and the security measures to protect their digital assets.

Building a Cryptocurrency Portfolio

As freelancers receive payments in cryptocurrencies, they have the opportunity to build a diversified portfolio. Instead of relying solely on traditional fiat currencies, freelancers can accumulate various digital assets. Keeping abreast of market trends and considering strategic conversions based on market conditions can optimize the value of the crypto portfolio.

Managing Cryptocurrency Volatility

Cryptocurrency markets are known for their volatility, which can impact the value of earnings. Freelancers should be cognizant of this volatility and consider strategies such as timely conversions to stablecoins or fiat currencies to mitigate the impact of market fluctuations. Utilizing financial tools like hedging or setting predetermined conversion points can add an extra layer of risk management.

Promoting Crypto Expertise

Crypto freelancers can leverage their proficiency in blockchain technology, cryptocurrency trading, or related fields to attract clients with specific needs in the crypto space. Highlighting expertise in areas like smart contract development, blockchain consulting, or crypto content creation can set freelancers apart in a competitive market.

Staying Informed about Regulations

The regulatory landscape for cryptocurrencies varies globally. Freelancers engaged in crypto freelancing should stay informed about the legal implications, tax obligations, and regulatory requirements in their respective jurisdictions. Compliance with local regulations ensures a smooth and lawful freelancing experience.

Conclusion

In conclusion, crypto freelancing represents a dynamic avenue for skilled individuals to offer their services in exchange for cryptocurrencies. By embracing platforms that support digital currency transactions, setting competitive rates, and navigating the nuances of cryptocurrency payments, freelancers can tap into a borderless and decentralized gig economy. As the adoption of cryptocurrencies continues to grow, crypto freelancing stands as a testament to the evolving nature of work and compensation in the digitalMarketing

Navigating the Crypto Ecosystem: A Guide to Crypto Affiliate Marketing

Crypto affiliate marketing provides individuals with a lucrative opportunity to participate in the cryptocurrency space by promoting products or services and earning commissions on successful referrals. This article delves into the dynamics of crypto affiliate marketing, exploring how enthusiasts can leverage affiliate programs to generate income in the ever-evolving world of digital assets.

Understanding Crypto Affiliate Marketing

Crypto affiliate marketing involves promoting cryptocurrency-related products or services through unique affiliate links. Affiliates earn commissions for every successful referral or sale generated through their promotional efforts. This form of marketing serves as a symbiotic relationship between product/service providers and affiliates, allowing both parties to benefit from the affiliate's promotional activities.

Choosing Crypto Affiliate Programs

Numerous cryptocurrency exchanges, wallets, trading platforms, and services offer affiliate programs. Popular examples include Coinbase, Binance, and Ledger. Affiliates should choose programs that align with their audience and interests. Factors to consider include commission structures, payment methods, and the reputation and reliability of the affiliate program.

Promoting Crypto Products and Services

Affiliates employ various strategies to promote crypto products or services. Content creation, such as blog posts, articles, or videos, can be an effective way to educate the audience and encourage engagement. Social media marketing, email campaigns, and SEO optimization are additional channels for reaching potential customers. Creativity and strategic promotion play key roles in maximizing affiliate marketing success.

Utilizing Affiliate Links and Tracking

Upon joining an affiliate program, affiliates receive unique tracking links that identify their referrals. These links are embedded in promotional content, and when users click on them and complete desired actions (e.g., signing up, making a purchase), the affiliate is credited with the referral. Ensuring proper implementation and tracking of these links is crucial for accurate commission attribution.

Understanding Commission Structures

Crypto affiliate programs offer various commission structures. Some programs provide a percentage of the referred user's transaction fees, while others offer fixed-rate commissions. Additionally, multi-tiered programs reward affiliates not only for their direct referrals but also for referrals made by individuals they've recruited into the affiliate program.

Navigating Compliance and Regulations

Affiliates operating in the cryptocurrency space should be aware of regulatory requirements and compliance standards. Adhering to local and international regulations helps prevent legal issues and ensures ethical marketing practices. Familiarizing oneself with disclosure requirements and the legal aspects of promoting financial products is essential.

Optimizing Conversions and Engagement

Affiliates aim to optimize conversions by creating compelling and informative content that resonates with their audience. Calls-to-action, promotional offers, and highlighting unique selling points can contribute to higher conversion rates. Engaging with the audience through forums, social media, or direct communication fosters trust and encourages users to act on affiliate recommendations.

Tracking and Analyzing Performance

Successful crypto affiliate marketers regularly track and analyze the performance of their campaigns. Monitoring metrics such as click-through rates, conversion rates, and commission earnings provides valuable insights. This data enables affiliates to refine their strategies, focus on high-performing channels, and adapt to changing market dynamics.

Conclusion

In conclusion, crypto affiliate marketing serves as a dynamic avenue for individuals to participate in the cryptocurrency ecosystem while earning commissions through promotional efforts. By strategically choosing affiliate programs, creating engaging content, adhering to compliance standards, and optimizing performance, affiliates can unlock the potential for generating income in the ever-expanding world of digital assets. As the cryptocurrency market continues to evolve, crypto affiliate marketing remains a resilient and innovative channel within the broader landscape of digital marketing.